The Dreyfus Affair: The History and Legacy of France's Most Antisemitic Political Scandal

By Charles River Editors

Captain Alfred Dreyfus

About Charles River Editors

Charles River Editors is a boutique digital publishing company, specializing in bringing history back to life with educational and engaging books on a wide range of topics. Keep up to date with our new and free offerings with this 5 second sign up on our weekly mailing list, and visit Our Kindle Author Page to see other recently published Kindle titles.

We make these books for you and always want to know our readers' opinions, so we encourage you to leave reviews and look forward to publishing new and exciting titles each week.

Introduction

An 1898 board game about the Dreyfus Affair

The Dreyfus Affair

"By my forty years of work, by the authority that this toil may have given me, I swear that Dreyfus is innocent. By all I have now, by the name I have made for myself, by my works which have helped for the expansion of French literature, I swear that Dreyfus is innocent. May all that melt away, may my works perish if Dreyfus be not innocent! He is innocent. All seems against me — the two Chambers, the civil authority, the military authority, the most widely-circulated journals, the public opinion which they have poisoned. And I have for me only an ideal of truth and justice. But I am quite calm; I shall conquer. I was determined that my country should not remain the victim of lies and injustice. I may be condemned here. The day will come when France will thank me for having helped to save her honor." - Émile Zola

Sometime in 1889, a woman named Madame Marie Bastian was recruited as an agent of the secretive "Statistical Section," an espionage and counter-intelligence agency attached to the military intelligence office of the French General Staff. Mme. Bastian, a cleaner employed by the German Embassy in Paris, and thanks to her Romany origins, she was somewhat acquainted with Germany and marginally conversant in the German language. She enjoyed complete and unrestricted access to the private residences of many important German diplomats and functionaries, and as she gathered up the torn-up documents in the various waste paper baskets, she routinely passed them on to a handler attached to the Statistical Section. Most of what was delivered was of little interest or importance, but on some occasions, documents taped back together and translated proved to be of significant value.

In September 1890, among a pile of torn-up documents delivered by Mme. Bastian was found a note handwritten in French which, when pieced together, proved to be a list of French military secrets handed over to the Germans by an unknown French officer of the General Staff. This discovery, which proved the existence of a traitor in the department, triggered a ferment in the corridors of the *Conseil Supérieur de la Guerre*, and the hunt was on for the culprit.

At that time, the French military establishment, along with the wider nationalist movement, was locked in a state of paranoia and internal disorganization as a consequence of France's catastrophic defeat at the hands of the Germans in the Franco-Prussian War of 1871. Tensions continued to exist between the two countries, and the broader issue of German spying tended to absorb a disproportionate share of the energies of both the local press and the General Staff, so the news, when it broke that a French officer was selling secrets to the Germans, rocked the foundations of the French intelligence community. The document in question came to be known as the "bordereau," or a "list" of military secrets for sale.[1]

By a process of elimination, officers of the military intelligence were able to narrow down a list of probable traitors, among whom was a young Jewish staff officer, Captain Alfred Dreyfus, who was immediately earmarked as the chief suspect. Dreyfus' handwriting was compared to that on the bordereau, and although the various handwriting experts who conducted the comparison failed to reach a common consensus, it was nonetheless judged that Dreyfus was indeed the culprit. In December 1894, Dreyfus was court-martialed, convicted, and sentenced to a term of life in prison. On January 5, 1895, in a formal parade, Captain Dreyfus was stripped of his rank, his sword was broken over the knee of a sergeant, and he was shipped overseas to the penal colony of Devil's Island on the coast of French Guiana.

According to most assessments of the age, France was not typically home to the systematic, "scientific" anti-Semitism that had such deep roots in Germany, and even more so further east in Russia and its dependencies. As proof of this, when the region of Alsace-Lorraine was annexed to Germany in the aftermath of the Franco-Prussian War, a majority of Jews of the region opted to leave in order to remain under the protection of France. While most of the early accounts of the Dreyfus Affair were polemic and sensational, pushing the anti-Semitic narrative, later historians have tended to observe that, initially at least, Dreyfus' Jewishness did not play a large part in his identification as the most likely suspect. Investigation of the matter was clumsy to say the least, and it was upon only the vaguest circumstantial evidence that the initial arrest was made. Dreyfus was, by all accounts, unpopular among his fellow officers, both Jew and Gentile, and in combination with various circumstantial factors, and a superficial handwriting comparison, it was this that pushed his name to the fore. However, once the Affair began to

---

[1] *Bordereau* is defined as "a detailed memorandum, especially one in which documents are listed."

gather momentum, and began to capture the attention of the wider French public, anti-Semitism undoubtedly became central to the evolution of events.

Dreyfus himself, a soft-spoken, prematurely balding man of 36, passionately maintained his innocence, and when he was arrested and taken into custody, he was utterly stupefied. The general public tended to follow the direction of the military, and virtually no voice was raised in his defense. His brother, Mathieu Dreyfus, and his wife Lucie were alone in supporting him and declaring his innocence, and the two retained the services of Edgar Demange, a prominent French lawyer famous for gaining an acquittal on behalf of Prince Pierre Bonaparte, charged with the 1870 killing of the Republican Victor Noir. As Alfred Dreyfus boarded a French naval cruiser destined for the coast of French Guiana, his lonely appeal faded with him, and for five years, his brother Mathieu and wife Lucie, with the help of Demange, labored tirelessly to win a retrial. In the meanwhile, the press and the general French public quickly forgot about him.

These are the essential facts of the "Dreyfus Affair," as it came to be known, an episode that in many respects defined French anti-Semitism in the late 19th century. A case was built with the central objective of protecting the integrity of French military establishment, and in the process, the relatively muted anti-Semitism in France (at least compared to other European nations) was transformed into an era of virulent and violent Jew-hatred that characterized and sullied the final decade of the 19th century in France. Even today, as many of the affair's nuances and facets have faded from memory, its political importance and anti-Semitic elements continue to be well-known and quite relevant today.

The Dreyfus Affair: The History and Legacy of France's Most Notorious Antisemitic Political Scandal examines the chain of events that produced one of the most notorious episodes in modern French history. Along with pictures depicting important people, places, and events, you will learn about the Dreyfus Affair like never before.

The Dreyfus Affair: The History and Legacy of France's Most Notorious Antisemitic Political Scandal

French Society Before the Dreyfus Affair

"Jews, vomited from the ghettos of Europe, are now installed as masters of the historic houses that evoke the most glorious moments of ancient France…Jews are the most powerful agents of disorder the world has ever seen." – Édouard Adolphe Drumont

In the early 1870s, the French were comprised of mostly the working class, with as many as 500,000 earning their bread and butter as industrial laborers alone. For decades, the disgruntled laborers protested against government-sanctioned injustices, among them the lopsided taxation system. They voiced their anxieties regarding the disproportionate distribution of wealth and expressed their discontent with the corruption that was rife within the rigged system, yet time and time again, their objections fell on deaf ears. By the humiliating end of the Franco-Prussian War, which took a toll on the already bleeding finances of many, the working class decided they would be silenced no longer.

The Third Republic, which prepared to take the reins following the signing of the armistice, was suspiciously abundant in royalists. Fearing the revival of monarchism and feeling betrayed by what they deemed the cowardice of the armistice signers, 2 million Parisians, a majority of whom were workers and students, rallied behind the Commune, a democratically elected socialist government that promoted policies shaped by Marxist and First International ideals. It was, as described by some historians, the "first truly democratic government in all of France," a government operated by "radicals" who led "the first working-class revolt." The Commune was backed by members of the National Guard, which staved off the French army and grappled for command of the city's government buildings and munitions. The National Guard succeeded in securing the government buildings and munitions on March 18, 1871, marking the start of the Commune's rule.

The Commune remained in power for about two months, and though it was always controversial, it was founded with good intentions. The autonomous council, or "Communards," as they called themselves, consisted of 60 members, all of whom held equal power. They were from all walks of life, including laborers, businessmen, scholars, journalists, and so on. From the start, the Communards retired the law of compulsory enlistment, discontinued the death penalty, and declared the separation of church and state, which meant that religion was no longer a required component of school curricula. In the same vein, church-owned estates became public property. The council also issued socialist policies that evened out the playing field for all classes across the board, reversing several privileges that unfairly oppressed those in the lower echelons.

To the dismay of the Commune's adherents, its existence was short-lived, largely due to incessant assaults by the French army. On May 21, 1871, the army descended upon Paris, massacred 20,000 Parisians, and replanted the flag of the Third Republic. 750 soldiers were killed in the melee as the Communards and the National Guard assembled makeshift barricades and did their best to fend off the soldiers, but their efforts were to no avail. They were left with no choice but to raise the white flag just one week later, signaling the dissolution of the Commune.

At the end of the entire affair, just about everyone's hands were stained with blood. On May 24, Communard Théophile Ferré ordered the execution of six high-profile prisoners, including Archbishop of Paris Georges Darboy. Following the surrender of the Communards, another 38,000 were taken hostage, and more than 7,000 were deported by the army under orders from the Third Republic. Those who were forcibly relocated were ultimately given the longer end of the stick, for many of those imprisoned were mercilessly put to death in a rampage now referred to as Semaine Sanglante ("Bloody Week"). Ferré himself was ultimately executed.

Ferré

Thus, France in the 1890s was defined by the Third Republic, and in general, the closing decades of the 19th century saw France embroiled in political turbulence and uncertainty, with multiple opposing forces – socialists, anarchists, monarchists and republicans – pulling in different directions and existing in a constant and deep state of mutual antipathy. Successive governments were weak, and the nation was buffeted and disturbed by multiple political, social, and economic upheavals.

That said, it's only fair to note that French society was not regarded as manifestly anti-Semitic, and certainly not to the same degree as France's eastern neighbors. After all, France had been the first European country to award full citizens' rights and legal equality to Jews. Jews had not played prominent roles in any of the great events and upheavals following the French Revolution, such as the humiliating defeat against the Prussians, so few people pointed the finger at Jews for the many problems that France was facing during this period.

This was in part thanks to a tendency of French Jews to display strong patriotism, if only to avoid potential discrimination. One of them was Alfred Dreyfus, who had fled Alsace-Lorraine when it was annexed by the German Empire and outwardly demonstrated his patriotism. France's Jews also showed interest in assimilating into what was a generally secular society. This differed quite noticeably from the separate social existence and cultural differences Jews experienced in Germany and Russia. Jews integrated more willingly into French society than Germany or Russia, attracted perhaps by its liberalism and sophistication, and in stark contrast to Germany and Russia, the French armed forces willingly recruited Jewish officers. Indeed, at the time that the Dreyfus Affair began to capture public attention, there were about 300 Jewish officers serving in the ranks of the armed forces, and 10 of them were generals.

At the same time, French liberalism freed many Jews from the stifling religious orthodoxy of Eastern Europe, and conversions to Christianity were not infrequent. Indeed, many traditional French Catholics also reveled in the same freedom from orthodoxy, seemingly heralding the dawn of a new age of enlightenment, secularism, and rationalism.

All of this had the effect of promoting an immediate and noticeable upward mobility among Jews, who subsequently became more influential in the fields of economics, finance, and politics by the late 1880s and 1890s. In hindsight, given the knowledge of what happened across Europe in the 20th century, the effects of this were predictable. The profiles of French Jews were redefined quickly, reintroducing what some began to see as disproportionate Jewish involvement in the affairs of state and the economy. From this, inevitably, the first seeds of institutionalized anti-Semitism began to sprout.

As general anti-Semitic sentiments began to grow, French monarchists, a powerful presence in the aftermath of the Second Empire, became increasingly dismayed with the Third Republic, which in their eyes was nothing more than a temporary expedient. Republicans gradually replaced monarchists in the government and bureaucracy, pushing a traditionalist and disgruntled class out of authority, at least in civil society. However, monarchists remained well represented in the officer class of the army, one of the few avenues of career advancement still open to them. This would have a major impact on the Dreyfus Affair.

Against this backdrop, the identification of Alfred Dreyfus as the key suspect in the drafting of the bordereau followed a clear logic, and it was not an effort to frame a Jewish officer, at least not in the beginning. At the time, Dreyfus was an academy officer on the General Staff, and among only a handful of men with direct access to the material revealed in the bordereau. It is also true that a superficial examination his handwriting indicated it certainly did resemble that upon the bordereau, and in the absence of technical examination, the belief that he was the author of the document was a fair conclusion to reach. It was only after various handwriting experts were unable to conclusively determine whether Dreyfus was indeed the author of the document, and thus categorically prove his guilt, that things became rather spurious. After that, a tranche of obscure documents appeared after being gathered by military intelligence, and their contents apparently implicated Dreyfus. One contained a reference to a spy on the General Staff who used the initial "D." Who produced them became something of a mystery.

A picture of the bordereau

Ultimately, the evidence presented to indict and convict Dreyfus was flimsy at the very best, and modern readers are left with the impression that there was a rush to judgement mainly as a vindication of the military establishment itself. Later accusations of anti-Semitism came about mainly because it was suggested that by accusing and convicting a Jew, it would be possible for the military establishment to claim that the traitor was "not one of us." The first substantial history of the affair, *Histoire de l'Affaire Dreyfus,* written in seven volumes by French author and politician Joseph Reinach, himself a Jew and a passionate supporter of Dreyfus throughout the saga, portrayed a deeply rooted culture of anti-Semitism in the French armed forces. The most widely read English version of the same story, *Captain Dreyfus: The Story of a Mass Hysteria*, written by another Jew, Nicholas Halasz, also tends to drive home the notion that institutionalized anti-Semitism lay very much at the heart of the Dreyfus Affair.

Though these accounts now tend to jibe with more modern accounts of the Dreyfus Affair, they were also intentionally polemical and one-sided, serving as elaborate propaganda pieces written at a time when Jews were beginning to find their voice in Europe. At the time, the modern Zionist movement, formally founded by the Hungarian Jewish journalist and activist Theodor Herzl in 1897, was beginning to gather strength. Herzl, as a journalist and a deeply interested observer, took away from the Affair a clear sense that even France, the most tolerant society in Europe, was susceptible to anti-Semitism, and that when push came to shove, the French would have the same essential response as every other European state. The Dreyfus Affair thus seemed like a clear indication that Jews would never be free of such persecution until a Jewish homeland was established.

Modern historians almost universally note that Dreyfus had a tendency to be smug, self-satisfied, and quite willing to flaunt the family wealth that liberated him from the same petty concerns about money that plagued his fellow officers. It's also worth noting that his fellow officers were mostly Catholic, educated, urbane and socially alert. They were drawn in the main from the impoverished nobility, the "monarchists and Bonapartists" who not only harbored traditional antipathy towards Jews but also Protestants of any color, as well as liberals, free-thinkers, intellectuals, and foreigners in general.

Regardless of whether anti-Semitism initially provided a motive for the accusations hurled at Dreyfus, it sure seemed to drive the subsequent and at times pathological determination on the part of the military establishment to gain and secure a conviction on the basis of evidence that even the most right-wing French publications were apt to question. Dreyfus' military record was exemplary, he was frequently promoted, and it was an article of faith within the officer corps of the French military, in keeping with the revolutionary mantra of *Liberté, Egalité, Fraternité*, that race, color, religion or creed would not influence or have any bearing on the career of an army officer.

Who Was Alfred Dreyfus?

"I was only an artillery officer, whom a tragic error prevented from pursuing his normal career. Dreyfus the symbol is not me." – Alfred Dreyfus

Alfred Dreyfus was born on October 9, 1859, the youngest of Raphaël and Jeannette Dreyfus' nine children. Raphael was a successful and wealthy industrialist, but in 1870, when the Franco-Prussian War broke out, 10-year-old Alfred and his family, along with many other wealthy,

French-speaking residents of Alsace, the easternmost province of France, moved west.

At the age of 19, he enrolled at the prestigious military school, the *Ecole Polytechnique,* and a year later he was appointed to the French artillery regiment with the rank of Captain. That was, in and of itself, clear testimony to his dedication and ability. In April 1890, he was enrolled in *Ecole Supérieure de la Guerre*, France's premier military academy, and he graduated the following year with honors. Within days of his graduation, he married his long-time fiancée Lucie Hadamard, the daughter of a wealthy Parisian diamond merchant.

At the age of 32, Dreyfus was granted a probationary appointment on the General Staff, attached to military intelligence. He later wrote, "The path of a brilliant career lay open before me, the future appeared under the best possible light. After the day of work, I enjoyed the rest and charms of familial life. We were perfectly happy, a first child brightened our home; I had no material cares, the same deep affection united me both to my own family and that of my wife."

Dreyfus' journey to this point was not without the occasional brush with institutionalized anti-Semitism. The story is told of a member of his examination panel who assessed his final performance giving him low marks for *cote d'amour*, which is simply "likeability," on the basis of his belief that Jews were generally unwelcome on the General Staff. Dreyfus subsequently lodged a complaint with the director of the school, and though sympathy was expressed to his plight, he was told that nothing more could be done.

However, there are many other assessments, both formal and informal, that, while acknowledging Dreyfus' talent and ability, also recorded clear criticism of certain aspects of his nature and personality. This tends to suggest that while Dreyfus was indeed a talented staff officer, his belief that he was being discriminated against might have stemmed from the fact that he was a difficult personality who was neither loved or admired by his fellow officers. Indeed, he was described by American Jewish historian Albert Lindemann, in his book *The Jew Accused: Three Anti-Semitic Affairs*, as "a loner, even among Jews, and a single-minded, spit-and-polish, strictly-by-the-book kind of officer, little interested in bonhomie and after-hours comradeship or even the social climbing that absorbed many other wealthy French Jews of the day." Lindemann also makes the point that Dreyfus, notwithstanding great "physical and psychic tenacity," was pedestrian in outlook, stiflingly conventional, and demonstrably patriotic. It would appear that his only source of companionship and the only recipients of his affection were his wife and their two children, Jeanne and Pierre.

Historians also report on rumors of Dreyfus' infidelities and womanizing, which was not in and of itself behavior likely to provoke the animus of his fellow officers, but simply that he was wealthy and able to indulge and boast of his indulgences more liberally and more frequently than they could.

As a result, when he was arrested, there were virtually no fellow officers prepared to immediately rally to his defense, and no doubt his aloof manner and generally disagreeable character made it easier for the initial charges to stick. In the trials that followed, the animosity shown towards him by many of his fellow officers came as a surprise, even as he kept holding on to a poorly placed faith in his senior officers.

The Trial

"You must live for the children. Think of the good years we have had together and the ones we shall have again. We will fight together." – Alfred Dreyfus to his wife Lucie

On October 15, 1894, Captain Dreyfus was formally indicted for treason, and in a state of utter bewilderment and confusion, he was thrown into a cell in the French military prison of Cherche-Midi. Although his house and those of his relatives and friends were searched and ransacked, no further incriminating evidence was unearthed. His wife was warned to keep silent on the matter in case she further compromised her husband's situation.

Dreyfus was told that he faced unimpeachable charges of treason, and he was offered a revolver in order that he might take the honorable way out, which he refused. While he swore with a passion that he was innocent and that a ghastly mistake had been made, his early interrogators, reporting back on his behavior, remarked that he appeared guilty.

Dreyfus in 1894

Le Petit Journal

SUPPLÉMENT ILLUSTRÉ

Le Petit Journal
Le Supplément Illustré

Huit pages : CINQ centimes

ABONNEMENTS

DIMANCHE 20 JANVIER 1895

ALFRED DREYFUS DANS SA PRISON

An 1895 depiction of Dreyfus in prison

News of Dreyfus' arrest was quickly picked up by the press, at which point his guilt became *de facto* in the eyes of the general public, and so relentlessly did the press pursue that narrative that any chance of proving the contrary quickly flew out the window. In this atmosphere, even the French Jewish community did not immediately rally to Dreyfus' defense. Herzl, who would later cite the effect of the Dreyfus Affair in his decision to found the Zionist movement, initially kept his distance. Although there were certainly some who presumed Dreyfus was guilty, most were more circumspect, and rather than voice any particular position, faith was placed in the likelihood that his innocence or guilt would be established by court-martial. What utterances were heard from the Jewish community tended to be placatory, anodyne, and carefully crafted to avoid any risk of blaming or offending the military. Few were willing to court controversy, and few indeed saw any value in a long and protracted controversy about a Jewish traitor.

Leading up to Dreyfus' court-martial, the press kept up a steady drumbeat of accusations and certainty, and no small amount of anti-Semitic rhetoric. The latter was expressed often in hysterical accusations against the Jewish officer corps as a whole, claiming they were committing treachery and espionage. From the onset, therefore, the omens were not auspicious for Dreyfus. This was compounded by the fact that the military was mortified and humiliated by the entire episode, and the more public attention the Affair gained, the more uncomfortable the situation became. Whether playing into the growing anti-Semitic fervor or being part of it, a successful trial and conviction of Alfred Dreyfus seemed to matter much more in the moment than any quest for the truth.

As a result, long before he stood before a court-martial, Alfred Dreyfus was tried and convicted in the public arena, even in his own constituency. The Jews of France sensed the prudence of keeping their mouths shut and hoping that the whole business would fade away as quickly as possible, and with as few repercussions as possible.

On December 19, 1984, a court-martial was convened at the Cherche-Midi prison, and for four days it sat and heard evidence. The *Conseil de Guerre*, the judging panel, comprised seven judges, each one a military officer who had been selected from every regiment other than the artillery (which happened to be Dreyfus' parent regiment). The president of the judging panel was Colonel Émilien Maurel, the commissary of the government was Major Brisset, and proceedings were held under conditions of strict secrecy.

The evidence presented was weak, and although the prosecution made no case alleging treachery by Jewish officers in general (knowing that this might provoke a public outcry), the suggestion remained implicit throughout, hanging over the entire proceeding like a dark cloud. The main article of evidence was the bordereau, which, in and of itself, fell far short of establishing guilt beyond a reasonable doubt. In the hands of a competent defense, it was pointed out that the military secrets listed in the document would not have concerned Dreyfus in the ordinary course of his work. Furthermore, mention was made in the document that the author was soon to leave for maneuverers, which quite obviously did not match Dreyfus' schedule.

A depiction of the trial

Although these anomalies were acknowledged by the prosecution, there was also a significant weight of circumstantial evidence backing up the prosecution's case. They pointed out that Dreyfus would certainly have been present in situations where access to such information was possible. This was supported by the sworn testimonies of various officers, which, while unverified, all supported the position of the prosecution in one way or another. Thus, the case was stitched together by a thread of suppositions that didn't establish concrete proof of Dreyfus' guilt but was certainly compelling and not unreasonable on its face.

The general view of the press and the public seemed to be that the trial was progressing better for the defense than the prosecution, and it was generally anticipated that Dreyfus would be acquitted. The main challenge for the prosecution lay in the inability of the various court-appointed handwriting experts to form a common opinion on the authorship of the bordereau, which was the central pillar of the prosecution. Then, the steady order of procedure was disturbed by the last-minute testimony of Commandant Hubert-Joseph Henry. Commandant Henry had already testified, but his second appearance was accompanied by a great deal of manufactured drama and emotion, during which he pointed his finger at Dreyfus across the gallery and declared, "The traitor! There he is." Moreover, he added a fact apparently neglected earlier, confirming the existence of a "secret informer," the identity of whom he would not disclose. This person had at some point identified Dreyfus as a German spy, which seemed to settle the matter, and Commandant Henry, a widely respected intelligence officer and a member of the Legion of Honour, was prepared to swear that this was the truth. At the last minute, this impassioned testimony, supporting what most present wished to believe, had a profound effect on the panel of judges.

Henry

Then, on the final day of the trial, the judges were handed a secret, sealed dossier, apparently originating from the Ministry of War. The contents had not been made known to the public or the defense. The dossier was not large, and what it contained remains unknown, but it has been speculated that some sort of fortifying testimony was contained within, for upon reading it, the mood in the courtroom changed. Leaks to the press were inevitable, and the likelihood of a guilty verdict began to emerge in newspaper accounts.

What is of most interest is the fact that the defense team was not permitted to view or be informed of the contents of the dossier, which was obviously in flagrant contravention of established legal precedents and certainly against French law, whether civil, criminal, or military. Upon the understanding that revealing the contents of the dossier might provoke a war with Germany, Demange's vigorous objections were brushed aside.

Demange

After that, the panel of judges retired, and it seems obvious that a unanimous decision of guilt had already been reached. On December 23, that pronouncement was made. Dreyfus was found guilty and sentenced to a term of life imprisonment on Devil's Island. It was further decided that Dreyfus should suffer public degradation, and in a now-famous ceremony, he was paraded before the general public and press. His sword was ceremonially broken, and his insignia of rank was torn off his uniform. As this was taking place, a steady chant of "Death to the Jews" could be heard from the crowd.

A contemporary depiction of the ceremony

A picture of the stripes ripped off of Dreyfus

That kind of chant was something that had been absent until then, and it seemed to many that the exposure of a Jewish traitor in the ranks of the intelligence services opened a floodgate of latent anti-Semitism in France which was at last permissible to express. Throughout the nation, as the news sunk in, there seemed to be a sense of satisfaction that a wealthy Jew had been exposed by the unimpeachable process of military justice. There was, indeed, precious little sympathy expressed in any quarter of French society for a man who had undergone a manifestly flawed judicial process, and who had been convicted on the most spurious grounds. French socialist leader Jean Jaurès, only much later a defender of Dreyfus, expressed at the time his regret that Dreyfus' crimes did not attract the death penalty. It was, moreover, his opinion that solidarity among military officers was the most likely reason for such leniency, backed up by widespread support and behind the scenes maneuvers on the part of the French Jewish community. No such thing was true, but that didn't stop Isadore Singer, a prominent French Jew who was editor of the *Jewish Encyclopedia* and founder of the *American League for the Rights of Man*, from asserting that Dreyfus should be punished according to the laws of Moses. That would have been death by stoning, with the first stone cast by the grand Rabbi of France.

The Matter Becomes an Affair

"If you shut up truth and bury it under the ground, it will but grow, and gather to itself such explosive power that the day it bursts through it will blow up everything in its way." – Émile Zola

After his conviction, Dreyfus was returned to his cell at the Cherche-Midi prison to await his transportation. He was held in isolation, unable to meet either with his family or his defense, but even before he stepped on board the ship that would carry him to Devil's Island, his brother Mathieu, his wife Lucie, and his lawyer Demange began plotting to void the conviction and win Dreyfus a new trial. It was, to be sure, a lonely quest – even among those who did not think Dreyfus was guilty, most were simply happy to see an end to the business. In general, the trial to date had not reflected well on the Jews of France, and now that the question of Jewish infidelity to France was so central to the story, it was in the interests of just about everyone for the dust to settle and for Alfred Dreyfus to disappear into the anonymity of Devil's Island. His family became social pariahs, especially among Jews, and as his brother bitterly observed that "not one hand was extended, every door was closed and those that knew us avoided us. We were plague-stricken."

Fortunately, the family had a lot of resources. Eschewing the press and any outside assistance, they leveraged the social gravitas of wealth to slowly build a front of sympathy. Mathieu was on one occasion taken to court by a senior military officer who believed that he had been offered a bribe, and during his trial, it was remarked in the press that this was simply another example of the Jews making nefarious use of their wealth.

Mathieu Dreyfus

Mathieu Dreyfus is often portrayed by most authors of the Dreyfus story as an impulsive and at times impetuous character who was nonetheless fanatically loyal to his brother. He was certainly not a popular or sympathetic figure, and his motives in this regard are rarely discussed. The bond of brothers certainly provided the impetus for his actions, but his fidelity to the Zionist cause was also important. He realized very quickly, perhaps under the influence of Lucie, who was no less fanatically loyal to her husband, that passive lobbying would achieve nothing when it came to the generally apathetic Jewish community. He needed to spread the message wider, and so the decision was made to abandon caution and begin agitating.

The most obvious avenue for this was the press, but caution was needed here too, for the press had already done critical damage to Dreyfus' cause, and going to the press might risk blowback on the Jewish community as a whole. France was teetering on the brink of war with Germany, and the Jews were widely believed, for no real reason, to be on the German side. Indeed, even as there was a small, but growing interest in Dreyfus' innocence over the coming years, the rest of his family remained ostracized among French society.

In the meanwhile, the issue gradually began to take on a political identity. Certain opposition politicians, for example, were discussing the possible advantage of accusing the Minister of War of an anti-Semitic conspiracy to convict an innocent man. It was a race issue which, rightly or wrongly, had the potential to embarrass the government. The government, in turn, girded itself to fight off any such accusations, and as a consequence, the issue became a political football for national party politics. All the while, Dreyfus himself sat in a fetid cell in the notorious French penal colony, and although, thanks to his wealth and class, he enjoyed greater privileges than most, he was kept ignorant of events and his correspondence was heavily censored.

Arria Belli's picture of the Dreyfus Tower on Devil's Island

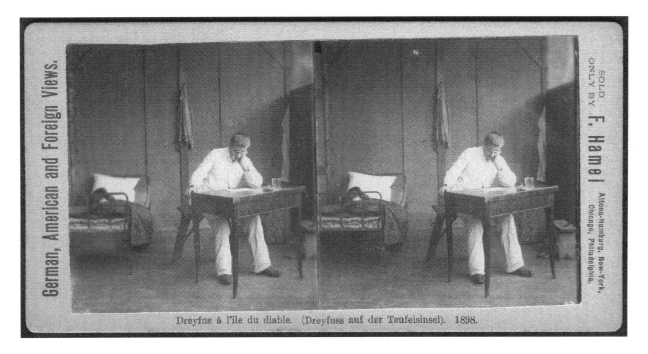

Dreyfus à l'île du diable. (Dreyfuss auf der Teufelsinsel). 1898.

An 1898 picture of Dreyfus in his room on Devil's Island

Things began to turn in 1896 when the role of the head of military intelligence was taken over by Colonel Marie Georges Picquart, later to be appointed French Minister of War. Picquart was among those mid-ranking officers involved in and deeply interested in the trial and conviction of Dreyfus. While it appears that he was generally prepared to accept Dreyfus' guilt, he remained troubled by the scarcity of hard evidence at the trial. Once the dust had settled, and once he had returned to his desk at the war ministry, he was surprised to observe that military secrets continued to be traded, which further heightened his concerns. His suspicions began to focus on Commandant Ferdinand Walsin Esterházy, a dissolute officer of intemperate habits who was mired in gambling debts. Picquart retrieved the notorious bordereau, compared it to a sample of Esterházy's handwriting, and was immediately struck by the similarity.

Picquart

Esterházy

This discovery marked a pivotal moment. Picquart was a by-the-book traditionalist and conservative military officer with no particular sympathy for the Jews. He had served as Dreyfus' instructor at General Staff training and was known to dislike him, as many others did. It is easy to imagine, then, that Picquart considered his suspicions, and what to do about them, very carefully indeed. He was now convinced that Dreyfus was not guilty, but he was also aware of the machinations of Mathieu, Lucie, and Demange. It concerned him a great deal that if he placed Esterházy in the spotlight, he might inadvertently be assisting them in unearthing a convenient "straw man." Nonetheless, once the decision was made in Picquart's mind to quietly begin building a case against Esterházy, he went about it with absolute determination.

Picquart has often been described as the hero of the great tragedy that was the Dreyfus Affair, with all of its ultimate devices of heroism and treachery, pathos and tragedy. Clearly, he took a tremendous risk to turn against the establishment in such an open and determined way, and for this, he certainly suffered. He later wrote, "The day will come when the truth will be understood by all, why public opinion was misled, why the criminals of the country were left unpunished."

Indeed, at the moment that news began to circulate through the General Staff that Picquart had "switched sides," so to speak, he was regarded and treated as an object of suspicion. There was some justification in this, for leaks of classified information began regularly finding their way into Demange's hands. Picquart seems to have taken the whole thing very much to heart, risking his career often as he engaged in regular overreach and not infrequent breaches of the law to try and build a viable case against Esterházy. Obviously, he was gambling his career and his liberty on proving Esterházy's guilt, for if he failed, he would certainly at some point stand before a court-martial himself. To get away with what he was doing, he would need to pull off a spectacular triumph of justice by proving Dreyfus's innocence or he may have well ended up joining Dreyfus on Devil's Island.

As Picquart was hard at work making a case against Esterházy, the honor of the military establishment worked with equal determination to counter him. Inevitably, he came under investigation, and for a while he was removed from the General Staff and transferred to Tunisia, where he languished safely out of the picture. However, even there he was not silent; he wrote a detailed dossier on his findings and ordered it to be opened in the event of his death, and moreover, he reported what he knew and what he suspected to any official person prepared or interested to listen. By this means he kept the matter alive, and as a consequence, a debate over the matter reentered the popular discourse.

As rumor begot rumor, and as more people began to sense a travesty of justice, a compelling case in the court of public opinion began to build against Ferdinand Esterházy. Esterházy did nothing to aid his own cause as he basked in his notoriety, his dissolute habits now public knowledge. As a braggart, he was on occasions prepared more or less to admit his guilt.

In the end, the military authorities were forced to sit up and take notice. Recognizing that some sort of court-martial was inevitable, it was decided to try the case quickly before any more compelling evidence could be amassed, and before Esterházy could implicate himself any more than he already had. The case compiled by Picquart, although intriguing, was weak, and the odds of an acquittal remained good.

Thus, on January 10, 1898, Esterházy was court-martialed, and after a brief hearing, the verdict was "not guilty." Once again, the army was vindicated, and French society could rest assured that a good and moral French Catholic officer had been saved from the evil machinations of the Jews.

The trial and prompt acquittal of Esterházy obviously had a profoundly demoralizing effect on the small corps of Dreyfus supporters, or "Dreyfusards," as they came to be known. The Dreyfusard movement was more widely supported than many realized, for it had captured the attention of the growing liberal movement. The French liberal establishment centered at that time around the arts, the theater, and Parisian literary circles, and while there were many in this group who expressed no particular love for the Jews, there were others who supported them in the new ideological spirit of equality and secularism.

Among the latter was the French stage actress, artist, author and impresario Sarah Bernhardt, who was a witness to the ceremony of degradation inflicted on Dreyfus. She was an early and vocal supporter of the Dreyfusard campaign, and she was a passive Jew herself, as were many others in the liberal-intellectual fraternity in Paris at the time. Another keenly interested observer was the French-Italian writer and novelist Émile Zola, who was emerging as an acclaimed literary voice, a spokesman of the era, and a staunch defender of many liberal and humanitarian causes. His novels and critiques were widely read, and he was a regular contributor to a popular French journal, *L'Aurore*, edited by the influential, independent Radical French politician Georges Clemenceau.

Bernhardt

Zola

Clemenceau

Clemenceau was another powerful ally to come over to the Dreyfusard cause. Initially, he was among those passionately convinced of Dreyfus' guilt, and the columns of his newspaper tended to reflect that position, but in the aftermath of the Esterházy trial, he felt obliged to change his mind. A keen politician, he was also among those who sensed a solid post upon which to flog a weak government, and with that, the tone of his reporting on the matter began to shift.

The key moment came when Émile Zola published a bitterly recriminatory article in *L'Aurore* entitled *J'Accuse...!* Published on January 13, 1898, *J'Accuse...!* was ostensibly an open letter addressed to the President of the Republic, and it became one of the greatest and most influential liberal manifestos in modern European history. In a sweeping and uncompromising tract, he openly accused various government ministers and prominent members of the General Staff of an open conspiracy to convict an innocent man. This, he claimed, was achieved through false evidence, secrecy, and a bogus trial. Zola even claimed that after Dreyfus' conviction, they suppressed new evidence that would have revealed his innocence.

Zola thundered:

"Ah, that first trial! What a nightmare it is for all who know it in its true details. Major du Paty de Clam had Dreyfus arrested and placed in solitary confinement. He ran to Mme Dreyfus, terrorized her, telling her that, if she talked, that was it for her husband. Meanwhile, the unfortunate Dreyfus was tearing his hair out and proclaiming his innocence. And this is how the case proceeded, like some fifteenth-century chronicle, shrouded in mystery, swamped in all manner of nasty twists and turns, all stemming from one trumped-up charge, that stupid bordereau. This was not only a bit of cheap trickery but also the most outrageous fraud imaginable, for almost all of these notorious secrets turned out, in fact, to be worthless. I dwell on this because this is the germ of it all, whence the true crime would emerge, that horrifying miscarriage of justice that has blighted France.

"The public was astounded; rumors flew of the most horrible acts, the most monstrous deceptions, lies that were an affront to our history. The public, naturally, was taken in. No punishment could be too harsh. The people clamored for the traitor to be publicly stripped of his rank and demanded to see him writhing with remorse on his rock of infamy. Could these things be true, these unspeakable acts, these deeds so dangerous that they must be carefully hidden behind closed doors to keep Europe from going up in flames? No! They were nothing but the demented fabrications of Major du Paty de Clam, a cover-up of the most preposterous fantasies imaginable. To be convinced of this one need only read carefully the accusation as it was presented before the court martial. How flimsy it is! The fact that someone could have been convicted on this charge is the ultimate iniquity. I defy decent men to read it without a stir of indignation in their hearts and a cry of revulsion, at the thought of the undeserved punishment being meted out there on Devil's Island. He knew several languages: a crime! He carried no compromising papers: a crime! He would occasionally visit his country of origin: a crime! He was hard-working, and strove to be well informed: a crime! He did not become confused: a crime! He became confused: a crime! And how childish the language is, how groundless the accusation!"

In the same vein, Zola pointed the finger at the panel of judges in both the Dreyfus and Esterházy trials, accusing them in each case of violating the law in order to find an innocent man guilty and a guilty man innocent. He wrote:

"It is said that within the council chamber the judges were naturally leaning toward acquittal. It becomes clear why, at that point, as justification for the verdict, it became vitally important to turn up some damning evidence, a secret document that, like God, could not be shown, but which explained everything, and was invisible, unknowable, and incontrovertible. I deny the existence of that document.... a document concerning national defense that could not be produced without sparking an immediate declaration of war tomorrow? No! No! It is a lie, all the more odious and cynical in that its perpetrators are getting off free without even admitting it. They stirred up all of France, they hid behind the understandable commotion they had set off, they sealed their lips while troubling our hearts and perverting our spirit. I know of no greater crime against the state…

"And now we come to the Esterhazy case. Three years have passed, many consciences remain profoundly troubled, become anxious, investigate, and wind up convinced that Dreyfus is innocent…

"Feelings were running high, for the conviction of Esterhazy would inevitably lead to a retrial of Dreyfus, an eventuality that the General Staff wanted at all cost to avoid…

"This must have led to a brief moment of psychological anguish. Note that, so far, General Billot was in no way compromised. Newly appointed to his position, he had the authority to bring out the truth. He did not dare, no doubt in terror of public opinion, certainly for fear of implicating the whole General Staff, General de Boisdeffre, and General Gonse, not to mention the subordinates. So he hesitated for a brief moment of struggle between his conscience and what he believed to be the interest of the military. Once that moment passed, it was already too late. He had committed himself and he was compromised. From that point on, his responsibility only grew, he took on the crimes of others, he became as guilty as they, if not more so, for he was in a position to bring about justice and did nothing. Can you understand this: for the last year General Billot, Generals Gonse and de Boisdeffre have known that Dreyfus is innocent, and they have kept this terrible knowledge to themselves?"

Zola concluded his famous piece with a series of accusations and a defiant vow:

"I accuse Lt. Col. du Paty de Clam of being the diabolical creator of this miscarriage of justice — unwittingly, I would like to believe — and of defending this sorry deed, over the last three years, by all manner of ludicrous and evil machinations.

"I accuse General Mercier of complicity, at least by mental weakness, in one of the greatest inequities of the century.

"I accuse General Billot of having held in his hands absolute proof of Dreyfus's innocence and covering it up, and making himself guilty of this crime against mankind and justice, as a political expedient and a way for the compromised General Staff to save face.

"I accuse Gen. de Boisdeffre and Gen. Gonse of complicity in the same crime, the former, no doubt, out of religious prejudice, the latter perhaps out of that esprit de corps that has transformed the War Office into an unassailable holy ark.

"I accuse Gen. de Pellieux and Major Ravary of conducting a villainous enquiry, by which I mean a monstrously biased one, as attested by the latter in a report that is an imperishable monument to naïve impudence.

"I accuse the three handwriting experts, Messrs. Belhomme, Varinard and Couard, of submitting reports that were deceitful and fraudulent, unless a medical examination finds them to be suffering from a condition that impairs their eyesight and judgement.

"I accuse the War Office of using the press, particularly L'Eclair and L'Echo de Paris, to conduct an abominable campaign to mislead the general public and cover up their own wrongdoing.

"Finally, I accuse the first court martial of violating the law by convicting the accused on the basis of a document that was kept secret, and I accuse the second court martial of covering up this illegality, on orders, thus committing the judicial crime of knowingly acquitting a guilty man...

"In making these accusations I am aware that I am making myself liable to articles 30 and 31 of the law of 29/7/1881 regarding the press, which make libel a punishable offence. I expose myself to that risk voluntarily...

"As for the people I am accusing, I do not know them, I have never seen them, and I bear them neither ill will nor hatred. To me they are mere entities, agents of harm to society. The action I am taking is no more than a radical measure to hasten the explosion of truth and justice...

"I have but one passion: to enlighten those who have been kept in the dark, in the name of humanity which has suffered so much and is entitled to happiness. My fiery protest is simply the cry of my very soul. Let them dare, then, to bring me before a court of law and let the enquiry take place in broad daylight! I am waiting."

Needless to say, the work was quite incendiary, and it pitched the French social and political establishments into a ferment. Zola's own work was all based on little evidence and a great deal of irresponsible guesswork, and no doubt most of it was untrue, but the effect of it was far greater than the sum of its parts, and it breathed new life into the Dreyfus trial, truly turning it into the "Dreyfus Affair." It stoked a roaring fire under the long-simmering pot of conspiracy, capturing the popular imagination and deeply embarrassing those named in the screed. Almost overnight, Alfred Dreyfus, entirely unaware of all of this on a faraway island, became a national *cause célèbre.*

Zola was both a critical and commercial success by the time he became embroiled in the Dreyfus Affair, and his work in the context of the times was regarded by the more intellectual and conservative elements of the Catholic right-wing in France as a symbol of the modern and corrupting trends overtaking the great imperial culture of France. Indeed, he was the champion of a debased secular culture behind which the seditious intellectual liberalism growing up amid the ruins of a greater age flourished. Like Picquart, Zola's audacity in defending a Jew and the uncompromising tone of his public utterances posed an inevitable risk to his career and his well-being, but nonetheless, the nation woke up, took notice of the moral issues pointed out, and began to talk.

As the start of the 20th century loomed, a strong thread of political and social liberalism was beginning to manifest in French society. The French overseas empire was undergoing a reconfiguration, and French society was becoming more humanitarian, conscience-laden, and inspired by the principals of equality, freedom, secularism and enlightenment. There were many who read and admired Zola but did not necessarily agree with his position. What impressed them most, however, was the fearless and unabashed manner in which the novelist took on the political and military establishment, the most powerful forces in republican France at the time. Despite their reservations over the question of Dreyfus' innocence, these people were nonetheless supporters, and they were, on the whole, representative of the academic classes, the intellectual and artistic avant-gardes, and the higher professions.

Obviously, Zola was aware of the risk, and he fully knew that virtually nothing he wrote could survive in a court of law. Those on the receiving end knew it too, and Zola was brought to court on charges of criminal libel and invited to provide proof to back up his accusations. What is perhaps interesting is that several prominent Parisian lawyers offered their services to the novelist pro bono, which gives some indication of the popular momentum that the issue had by then begun to accumulate. Meanwhile, the President of the French Bar, Henri du Buit, offered his services and defense counsel if Zola would only enter a plea of insanity.

In the end, Zola was tried twice. His first trial commenced on February 7, 1898, and with no expectation of a legal victory, he turned his court appearances into a platform to reinvigorate his case against the army. In that regard, he was obviously successful. The trial was a press bonanza, and through this coverage, Zola succeeded in convincing skeptics and further stigmatizing the military as a whole in the entire grubby episode. The political voices now articulating accusations against the army grew, and a great deal of discomfiture began to be felt in the administrative corridors of the General Staff.

Another interesting feature is the fact that Zola, like Picquart, was no great and enduring friend of the Jews. In fact, many of his works were populated by crude racial generalizations. Some of the most oft-quoted examples of this can be found in *L'Argent*, which included the following passage: "It is indeed Jewry as a whole, that stubborn and cold-blooded conqueror, marching towards the sovereign kingship of the world's nations, that it has brought, one by one, with its omnipresent gold."

Clearly, Zola was not waging a campaign in support of the Jews of France, nor was he simply fighting for justice. It was apparent he was launching an attack on the political establishment and the military, both worthy targets in his mind, and the Dreyfus Affair was a convenient cudgel in the endeavor. Thus, many scholars now believe that in Zola's eyes, the Dreyfus Affair was less a question of Jews and anti-Semitism as it was a contest between left and right in France.

Zola was found guilty of libel and convicted on February 23, 1898, after which his name was struck from the Legion of Honor. However, this was not the end of the matter, for his first conviction was overturned on a technicality, and he was retried on July 18 and again found guilty. This time, on the advice of his lawyer, he fled France for Britain, arriving in London on the overnight train with a single suitcase in his hand. What commenced then was a brief few months of unhappy exile from October 1898 to June 1899.

In the meanwhile, back in France, the divisions over the Dreyfus Affair began to polarize French society. Anti-Jewish riots broke out in cities across the republic, synagogues were routinely attacked, Jewish shops were looted, and Jews were assaulted in the streets. The authorities appeared ambivalent and at best ineffective, and many press reports lamented the arrival of Russianesque pogroms in the city streets of France. In Algeria, an overseas province of France where anti-Semitism was always much stronger, the response was even more violent and explosive.

In the weeks and months that followed, this initial reaction solidified into rolling anti-Jewish boycotts, while right-wing, anti-Semitic leagues were founded in various parts of the country. It is ironic that while Zola managed to renew interest and invigorate the entire Dreyfus Affair, he also succeeded in energizing and popularizing the anti-Semitic movements that had so conspicuously failed to achieve a mass following in years past. It all boded ill, not only for Dreyfus himself, still anonymously languishing in his island prison, but for the cause and safety of French Jewry as a whole. Herzl observed all of this and believed that the time had come for Jews to reevaluate France as the great Jewish sanctuary. Indeed, the last two years of the 19th century would come to be regarded as the peak of French anti-Semitism before World War I. Jews across the country quickly understood that their ability to achieve social mobility, and the willingness of Christian France to tolerate it, was rapidly coming to an end.

At the same time, there was a more liberal, rational reaction to the Affair that was also provoked by Zola's accusations and his subsequent trial, and it would prove to be of far greater significance. Again, the Dreyfusard movement was not necessarily driven by any positive sentiments towards the Jews or any sympathy for Dreyfus himself, but for the more elemental concerns that spoke to the middle classes, and the moderate voting public. There was, for example, a well-founded fear of the anti-republican, radical right, and a sense that public disorder might evolve into a class war or perhaps a *coup d'état*. For the left, it was an opportunity to discredit the right for its association and defense of such an obvious and flagrant miscarriage of justice.

The original unwillingness of the French moderates to give Dreyfus the benefit of the doubt arose from an entirely different set of fears. The Dreyfus Affair mounted a direct challenge against one of the most sacred and revered institutions of France, the military, which was weakened and unstable in the aftermath of the Franco-Prussian War. The army stood vanguard against the threat of class conflict, the rise of anarchism, the militant labor movement, and revolutionary socialists at war with the republican order. A strong, united, and supported military, as a bulwark against social revolution, was viewed by a moderate, republican bourgeoise as more important than the rights of one disgraced Jew.

Needless to say, a strong element of that moderate, republican bourgeoisie was the Jewish community itself, which was placed in a very difficult dilemma. Most Jews arrived in France and settled in relative peace under the essential protection of a social establishment committed to justice and equality for all. Even among those unconvinced of Dreyfus' guilt, the sacrifice of one Jew might not be too high a price to pay to protect France from external and internal threats, and letting Dreyfus go might shield French Jewry from any reprisals. It was only as insistent questions surrounding Dreyfus' trial, conviction, and sentence became too compelling to ignore that a significant number of middle-class Jews began to swing over towards open support for a retrial. None would go any further than that, and there were few open proclamations of Dreyfus' innocence originating from French Jews.

There also happened to be, among the more thoughtful elements of the political establishment, a sense that anti-Semitism had about it more than a passing hint of revolutionary socialism. It now appeared to represent an attack against the moneyed classes, evidenced by the fact that the socialist left did not immediately rally behind the Dreyfusards. They did so only when it became clear that they were losing prominence to the much more active right-wing radicals. Upon that, the left was inevitably obliged to react in a manner that contradicted the right, turning Dreyfus, a rich, Jewish military officer, into a socialist and left-wing icon.

Alongside these broader, societal shifts that brought the Dreyfus Affair into sharper focus, there were more practical matters of law and evidence that added to the increasingly obvious fact that Dreyfus was innocent. First and foremost, after he had fled France for England, Esterházy was now quite willing to admit to whoever asked that it was he who had authored the infamous bordereau. His confession was somewhat reluctantly received by the military intelligence department because Esterházy implied that his involvement had been part of a much wider espionage plot. According to Esterházy, the treachery involved officers much more senior than him, and many of them were still drawing army pay.

Furthermore, it was now clear that Commandant Henry, whose testimony had been so vital to the prosecution, had indeed committed forgery in an effort to shore up the army's case against Dreyfus. This discovery came in the wake of an investigation commissioned by the Ministry of War to try and suppress the issue, but when it was revealed and made public, the accusations further fueled a growing public demand to grant Dreyfus a retrial. After he was arrested and detained, Commandant Henry tearfully confessed his actions before he slashed his own throat.

By late 1898, the Dreyfusard movement had expanded and broken up into numerous factions, and expectations were high that some sort of denouement was pending. The matter was by then more political than moral, and with momentum behind them, the Dreyfus family continued to apply pressure. With significant expenditures, unrelenting lobbying, and appeals to the highest courts of the land, they were rewarded on June 3, 1899 when the Supreme Court of Appeal, the highest court in France, granted a *révision* and ordered that Dreyfus be given a new trial.

The news was quickly communicated to Devil's Island, where Dreyfus had languished in isolation for five years, largely remote from the political firestorm that his detention provoked. Within a few days, he was on board a ship bound for France, and on July 1, he landed anonymously on the Brittany coast before being spirited to Rennes, where his retrial was due to be held. Zola returned to France on June 4, and Picquart was released from prison on June 9.

On June 22, while Dreyfus was still on the high seas, a change of government in Paris ushered into power a committed Dreyfusard, Pierre René Waldeck-Rousseau, who was leading a center-left coalition government that was steadier on its platform than any previous Third Republic administration. He took a deep interest in the affair, and he was determined once and for all that it would be resolved in the interests of national security.

Waldeck-Rousseau

The theatrics were not quite over. The trial, which, when including the Esterházy and Zola trials, represented the fourth time the matter had been heard in a court of law, began on August 7, 1899 in Rennes, the regional capital of Brittany. Although fielding a case that was somewhat weakened by the Esterházy confession, the prosecution was nonetheless coherent, and the case was forcefully presented. New evidence was revealed, including additional testimony that Dreyfus had at some point confessed to the crime. Moreover, a clearer timeline was presented that indicated Dreyfus was present each time a leak of information occurred, allowing for the strong likelihood that he was responsible. The prosecution submitted a request through the German Embassy in Paris for German intelligence to testify, a request that was turned down, but in sum, the circumstantial evidence was presented as simply too overwhelming to be purely coincidental.

Adding to the momentum of the prosecution, Dreyfus' lawyers, Edgar Demange and Fernand Labori, appeared divided and ill-prepared, calling only some 20 witnesses to the prosecution's 70. Dreyfus, despite the fact his physical condition was clearly compromised after five years on Devil's Island, appeared cogent and completely fluent with the files of evidence produced in just a few weeks.

Again, the emotional elements of the trial seemed sometimes to overwhelm the cold pragmatism of law. Of the 70 prosecution witnesses, most were army officers who offered unwavering oral testimony against Dreyfus without offering any proof, while the confessions of

Esterházy and Henry were treated with derision and scorn. The anti-Dreyfusard front was led by General Auguste Mercier, who was Minister of War when the scandal of the bordereau broke. Mercier was the loudest voice at Rennes calling for a reconviction, and he kept up a steady drumbeat of press reportage, frequently promising fresh revelations even as nothing of the sort ever came to light. Mercier asserted, "My conviction since 1894 has not suffered the slightest damage, rather it is deepened by a more comprehensive study of the case, it is finally strengthened by the failure of the results obtained [from the Military Court] to demonstrate the innocence of the convicted, despite the huge number of millions spent foolishly."

Mercier

Demange and Labori

Dreyfus' legal defense was cobbled together rather at the last minute, and a damaging difference of opinion did indeed exist between the two principals. Demange wanted simply to gain an acquittal on behalf of Dreyfus, avoiding any push into the realm of politics, while Labori, brilliant and impulsive, argued for taking the offensive in order to soundly defeat and publicly humiliate the General Staff. On August 14, as he walked to the court for the mid-morning session, Labori was approached and shot in the back by an unknown assailant who was never found. He was hospitalized for a week, which perhaps worked more in Dreyfus' favor than not. When Labori returned to the courtroom, the contretemps with Demange continued, with Mathieu Dreyfus vainly trying to mediate.

What had been a scrappy, combative and generally untidy trial ended on September 9, 1899 with a predictably equivocal verdict. Dreyfus was convicted once again of treason, but this time with "extenuating circumstances," the character of which was not revealed. Under the code of military law, a panel of seven military judges voted five to two, which was one vote short of an acquittal.

Needless to say, those on either side of the issue found reason to be either outraged or jubilant, and in the immediate aftermath, the press expressed the views of each side with suitable passion. The anti-Dreyfusards expressed themselves generally satisfied with the verdict, although the sentence of 10 years imprisonment was regarded as excessively lenient. On the other hand, the

Dreyfusards outnumbered the anti-Dreyfusards, and dissatisfaction with the verdict was widely felt and widely expressed, in particular in government, where sympathy for Dreyfus was running high. The *New York Times*, reflecting the collective opinion of the international press, remarked in an editorial that the judges "looked more guilty that Dreyfus ever had."

With the nation so utterly exhausted by the Dreyfus Affair, it became a question of finding an accommodation that would satisfy all sides. The obvious answer was a presidential pardon, and to this end, Waldeck-Rousseau began tentative discussions with Dreyfus' inner circle of supporters. It was put to Dreyfus that a pardon would be granted if he would formally submit a petition, which carried with it the implication that wrongdoing was admitted. The admission would then require a pardon.

By this time, Dreyfus, having already endured five years of incarceration under the most rigorous conditions, could hardly face the possibility of returning, so he agreed to an extremely unpalatable compromise. The Dreyfusards, the "revisionists" who had for so long held firm in his corner, were deeply disappointed, while the anti-Dreyfusards held it up as a vindication of their rather untenable position. On September 19, 1899, Alfred Dreyfus was granted a formal pardon by the President of the Republic, Émile Loubet, and that seemed to be that. Two days later, the Minister of War, General Gaston de Galliffet, issued orders to the Army General Staff that the matter was henceforth to be considered closed, and in December 1900, an amnesty law was passed that excused all transgressions or indiscretions related to the Dreyfus Affair.

The international reactions to the verdict and the manner of Dreyfus' pardon were furious and sustained. Anti-French demonstrations broke out in an estimated 20 foreign capitals, and a barrage of press criticism was sustained for weeks. Numerous international boycotts were put into effect, while the Lord Chief Justice of England, Lord Russell of Killowen, who sat through the trial at Rennes as an observer, remarked, "The Military judges were not familiar with the law or criminal proceedings. They lacked the experience and skill that can see the evidence behind the evidence. They were drowning in prejudice and they acted according to what they saw as the honor of the army. Impressed, full of respect for their superiors, they accorded too much importance to fragile allegations that were only made against the accused."[2]

Of course, the outrage had to be taken with a grain of salt because the major powers in Europe were already moving towards a major war, and relations between France and Germany tended to supersede the legal or ethical merits of the case. A full exoneration of Dreyfus would amount to a full exoneration of Germany, which had, in many respects, been as much on trial throughout the scandal as Dreyfus himself. Relations between Germany and France, if not entirely normalizing, nonetheless relaxed somewhat in the aftermath of the Dreyfus Affair.

---

[2] *The Appeals Court in the Dreyfus Affair*, Guy Canivet, 2006 (in French), Quoting from: Report to Queen Victoria, Lord Russell of Killowen, 16 September 1899

Dreyfus after the Affair

The Dreyfus family in 1905

"During these first days, when, in the disarray of mind and senses which was the consequence of the iniquitous sentence passed on me, I had resolved to kill myself, my dear wife, with her undaunted devotion and courage, made me realize that it is because I am innocent that I have not the right to abandon her or willfully to desert my post>" – Alfred Dreyfus

Dreyfus, now released from prison and returned to his family, and somewhat under a cloud in the estimation of the Dreyfusards (now more of a political movement than a front for justice) for accepting his pardon, worked steadily towards a *révision* of the Rennes verdict and a complete exoneration. This would be made more difficult by the fact the matter inevitably faded from popular consciousness in France as the French hoped the entire business could finally be buried, but the French general election of 1902 saw a victory for the left via the reelection of the socialist Jean Jaurès, who held the office of Prime Minister between 1893 and 1898. Jaurès was a leading Dreyfusard during the height of the Dreyfus Affair, and for reasons of personal conviction and politics, he revived it, pointing at numerous inconsistencies in the Rennes trial that were subsequently brought up and examined by the press. This opened the door to a proper judicial investigation of the conduct of the Rennes trial, and the case in general, which now enjoyed considerable academic interest and political momentum. The investigation was led by the Minister of War, General Louis André, and it seems that for the first time the records of the Statistics Section of the General Staff, from where the scandal originated, were properly examined. With that, a trove of obviously fabricated and forged documents indicting Dreyfus were unearthed. There was obviously a political motive for all of this, but it revealed Dreyfus was almost certainly innocent, the victim of an overzealous and self-preserving military establishment eager to exonerate itself.

In November 1903, the investigating commission submitted its report to the Minister of Justice. This, in turn, prompted an official review conducted by another prominent lawyer, Ludovic Trarieux, which resulted in a great deal of to-and-fro before the French Supreme Court of Appeals. The case hung on several forged documents, particularly those surrounding the authorship of the bordereau. On March 9, 1905, an 800 page report was submitted by the Attorney General in which his office demanded that all convictions against Dreyfus be quashed without further appeal or reference to a court of law. In due course, on July 12, 1906, the Supreme Court of Appeals issued a unanimous cancellation of the judgment without further reference to the military trial at Rennes, pronouncing "the end of the rehabilitation of Captain Dreyfus." It continued, "Whereas in the final analysis of the accusation against Dreyfus nothing remains standing and setting aside the judgment of the Military Court leaves nothing that can be considered to be a crime or misdemeanour; therefore by applying the final paragraph of Article 445 no reference to another court should be pronounced."

The rehabilitation of Alfred Dreyfus carried with it political overtones no less obvious than every other phase of the Dreyfus Affair. His fall and subsequent rise spoke to the evolving institutionalization of anti-Semitism in France. At one time, the anti-Semitism was the main fuel of public demonstrations against him, and the same discrimination also led to passionate advocacy on his behalf. No doubt the public display of contrition that his rehabilitation implied would have been neither so public nor so forceful had not his status as a Jew been so central to the whole saga.

On July 13, 1906, at the age of 47, Alfred Dreyfus was reinstated in the French army with the rank of artillery major, which, under the normal course of promotion, backdated to 1903, would have been his likely status. It was an imperfect result since his five years of imprisonment was not taken into account in this reconstruction of his career. Dreyfus would likely have been promoted to the rank of Colonel if not for the case.

Major Dreyfus remained in uniform for only a year, serving out what was perhaps a symbolic term before he retired. He cited the recurrence of tropical fever and the strain on his health of five years under conditions of penal transport.

Even as Dreyfus went about living the rest of his life, the Dreyfus Affair continued to hang in the air, and as social and political tensions in Europe grew before World War I, it began to acquire a status somewhat more than the sum of its parts. The evolution of the Dreyfus Affair had less to do with Dreyfus himself than a battle between republicans and monarchists, left and right, modernists and traditionalists. It was fundamentally a battle between those on the left who supported the republic and those on the right who longed for a return to the "old order." The former were the Dreyfusards, and the latter were anti-Dreyfusards. The overarching theme of anti-Semitism now served to widen the ideological gap between the anti- and pro-republican movements, and it united both sides in opposition to one another. In other words, it sharpened the lines of division between two preexisting forces in France and brought the struggle between those sides into focus. As one writer put it, "The affair affected right-wing politics by uniting parties with totally different ideologies and by restoring hope of disintegrating the republic by changing public opinion and demanding a plebiscite in order to change the constitution and instate a more authoritarian government. It then subsequently affected the left-wing parties as they had to defend the attacks made on the republic by the right-wing media."[3]

Ultimately, the Dreyfus Affair symbolized a victory for the Republic in its struggle for legitimacy against the anti-republican movement. The main supporting institutions of the anti-republicans were the army and the church, and once it had been revealed that the army stood on the corrupt side of the affair and that the republicans stood as the champions of truth and virtue, the wind was effectively removed from the sails of the anti-republican movement. The military establishment was chastised and discredited. The long-established call for a plebiscite to challenge the legitimacy of the Third Republic withered away. The victory of the Republic over the reactionary, right-wing forces of the church and the army was consummated in 1905 by the formal separation of church and state, and the depoliticization of both the church and the army.

As for Dreyfus, a few notable events punctuated his retirement. In the summer of 1908, on the occasion of the transfer of the ashes of Zola to the Panthéon, the mausoleum of the great heroes of France, Dreyfus was shot and slightly wounded by an extreme right-wing journalist named Louis Grégori. This incident was a reminder of the powerful symbolism that the innocuous figure of Alfred Dreyfus still held on the polarized extremes of French politics.

Dreyfus remained a reserve officer in the French army, which meant that he returned to uniform upon the outbreak of World War I. Fighting for the country that had so thoroughly wronged him, Dryfus served in a staff capacity as the commander of an artillery depot and a supply column. In 1917, he was present on the front lines at the Chemin des Dames and Verdun. It has been noted by several historians that Dreyfus was the only French officer involved in the Dreyfus Affair who served during World War I, and after the war ended, he was elevated to the rank of Officer of the Legion of Honour in 1919. His son Pierre also served as an artillery

[3] Jacquet, Jean-Baptiste Tai-Sheng. *The Significance of the Dreyfus Affair on Politics in France from 1894 to 1906.* E-International Relations, June 6, 2012

officer, winning the *Croix de Guerre*.

Perhaps the most stirring irony was the fact that the frontline artillery piece used to meet the early German advances was the very one at the center of the controversy. Its unique design features, allowing for sustained accuracy under rapid fire, were those that Dreyfus was accused of selling to the Germans.

Dreyfus ended his military career at the rank of colonel, and he survived in reasonable health until July 12, 1935, when he died of apparent heart failure at the age of 75. His grandchildren donated over thousands of Dreyfus' personal documents and belongings to the Musée d'art et d'histoire du judaïsme ("Museum of Jewish art and history"), including letters, pictures, legal documents, and more. The display of Dreyfus artifacts serves as a stark reminder that the name of an obscure French officer remains instantly recognizable more than 120 years after his wrongful conviction caused a major uproar throughout the West.

Dreyfus in 1934

Online Resources

Other books about French history by Charles River Editors

Other books about the Dreyfus Affair on Amazon

Further Reading

McMillan, James F. Twentieth-Century France: Politics and Society in France 1898–1991 (1992) pp. 3–12

Sowerwine, Charles. France since 1870: Culture, Society and the Making of the Republic (2001) excerpt and text search pp. 67–72

Michael Burns, Rural Society and French Politics, Boulangism and the Dreyfus Affair, 1886–1900 Princeton University Press.

Alfred S. Lindemann, The Jew Accused: Three Anti-Semitic Affairs, Dreyfus, Beilis, Frank, 1894–1914 (Cambridge University Press).

Michael Burns, Dreyfus: A Family Affair, from the French Revolution to the Holocaust, New York: Harper.

Michael Burns, France and the Dreyfus Affair: A Documentary History (Boston: Bedford/St. Martin's)

Eric Cahm, The Dreyfus Affair in French Society and Politics New York: Longman

George R. Whyte, The Accused – The Dreyfus Trilogy, Inter Nationes, ISBN 3-929979-28-4

George R. Whyte, The Dreyfus Affair – A chronological history, Palgrave Macmillan 2006, ISBN 978-0-230-20285-6

Ruth Harris, The Assumptionists and the Dreyfus Affair, Past & Present (2007) 194#1 175–211. in Project MUSE

Ruth Harris, Dreyfus: Politics, Emotion, and the Scandal of the Century (Henry Holt and Company)

Philippe Oriol, History of the Dreyfus Affair – Vol 1 – The History of Captain Dreyfus, Stock, (ISBN 978-2-234-06080-7)

Louis Begley, Why the Dreyfus Affair Matters (Yale University Press)

Frederick Brown, For the Soul of France: Culture Wars in the Age of Dreyfus (Alfred A. Knopf)

Robert L. Fuller, The Origins of the French Nationalist Movement, 1886–1914, Jefferson, NC: McFarland.

Piers Paul Read, The Dreyfus Affair, Bloomsbury, London

Free Books by Charles River Editors

We have brand new titles available for free most days of the week. To see which of our titles are currently free, click on this link.

Discounted Books by Charles River Editors

We have titles at a discount price of just 99 cents everyday. To see which of our titles are currently 99 cents, <u>click on this link</u>.